A CARTOGRAPHY OF PEACE

A CARTOGRAPHY OF PEACE

JEAN L. CONNOR

PASSAGER BOOKS
Baltimore, Maryland
2005

FIRST EDITION
Published 2005 by Passager Books

ACKNOWLEDGMENTS
Grateful acknowledgment is made to the editors of the
following magazines in which these poems first appeared:
Comstock Review: "The Women"
Hunger Mountain: "Family Stories," "A Poem of December"
Passager: "Of Some Renown," "Overcast," "Late August,"
"Mutual," "Absence," "The Gift," "Seamless," "Neither Sun
Nor Moon"
Poetry Daily: "Mutual"
Yankee Magazine: "No Rain"

Special thanks to Mary Azrael and Kendra Kopelke,
without whom this book would not have been possible.

Library of Congress Cataloging-in-Publication Data
Connor, Jean L.
A Cartography of Peace / Jean L. Connor
ISBN 0-9631385-0-2
1. Literature 2. Poetry
2005903570

Passager Books is in residence at the University of
Baltimore in the School of Communications Design.

PASSAGER BOOKS
1420 North Charles Street
Baltimore, Maryland 21201
www.passagerpress.com

To Skip Renker, Valerie Graham,
and my friends at Wake Robin
And in memory of Charles Whiston,
Sam Prentiss and William Stafford

CONTENTS

I

II

III

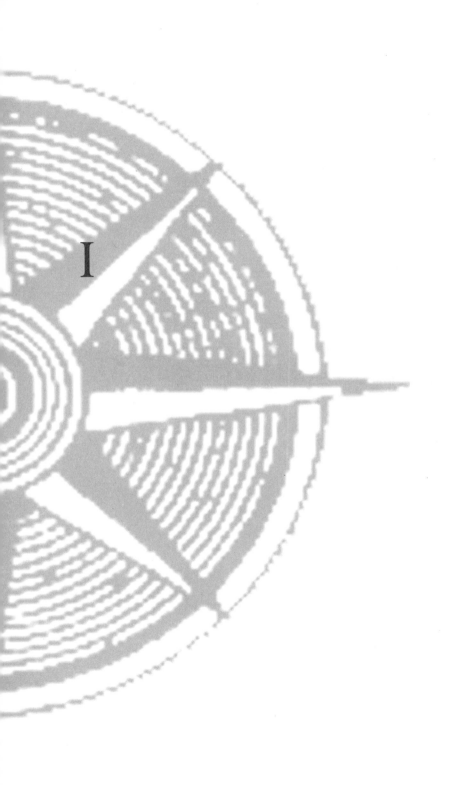

I

OF SOME RENOWN

For some time now, I have
lived anonymously. No one
appears to think it odd.
They think the old are,
well, what they seem. Yet
see that great egret

at the marsh's edge, solitary,
still? Mere pretense
that stillness. His silence is
a lie. In his own pond he is
of some renown, a stalker,
a catcher of fish. Watch him.

THE GIFT

You are young. You want bushels
of peonies, heady with fragrance,
arbor after arbor of roses,

bouquets of blue iris, fields
of red poppies, all in profusion,
after Monet. We do not have

them. We never possessed them.
Now our gathering baskets
are empty, except for a few

cosmos, spared from frost.
I'm happy, this late in
the season, to have flowers

to give you. Perhaps the glass
bud vase. The grace of the daisy-like
blossoms, wide white petals whorled

around gold centers; the feathery
foliage, delicate green; – even
three cosmos change a room.

AFTER VACATIONING IN MAINE

I have come home with two gray stones,
one flat, one round. I would hold
to their silence, their calm. I have come
home with two jars of blueberry jam

and one pint of wild blueberries
picked by a small boy on the barrens.
The sky wants to question
the sea and the sea wants to question

the sky, everything a question, except
for blueberries that only urge me
to eat. I have come home with one
postcard. I sent the other three.

Mountains. Ocean. Why should I think
of Yosemite after Maine? For no
reason, except there are landscapes
we cannot master. The rocks rise,

the waves break. No one asks,
"Is it Thursday? Is it Sunday?
Is it even today?" I have
come home with a small clay pot,

glazed black. Right for a few flowers,
no more. I turn the pot in the light.
It was to be a gift, but now it holds
the cove, the morning light on the water,

the hedges of roses, the cry
of wind-borne gulls, the heath,
a taste of blueberries. So
small a thing and overflowing.

LATE AUGUST

Everything was made of time:
the apples, green, the milk-weed pods,
split and drying, the seeds,
wind-borne, driven.

All was movement and becoming,
clouds cartwheeled through space,
never arriving. Day held
no fixed point, only urgencies

and the tattered banners
of the hours. At last,
the longed-for darkness came,
hollowed out, shaped as night.

Then, not as an intruder,
but as one accustomed to the place,
the hour, a cricket began to sing,
steady, sure, and as he sang

the world slowed to meet
his pace, found itself webbed
about in peace. The grasses —
sleep-heavy, wet with dew.

FAMILY STORIES

How easy the dead sit among us,
clothed in a self, apt and true.
No need for denim, corduroy or twill.

Old jokes please them, new ones,
too. They listen while we tell
stories of summers past – the rented pony

that ran away, the time we built
a lean-to in the woods and everyone
itched with poison ivy. The dead

are free to come or go,
but we invite them.
Their possessions float

free, too, as in a painting by Chagall,
suffused in a warm and tender light,
part love song, part folk tale,

but real enough. Even now,
my uncle's cuckoo clock,
long since lost, is faithful

to its task. Precisely on the hour,
the cuckoo opens his little door,
makes his proclamation, if I ask.

How fortunate we are in the dead,
here among us, already knowing
all that we long to tell them.

THE TOWN WHERE THEY LIVE

A grandfather who grows roses,
or an uncle who prefers his peas
simmered in milk, may be real,

but the town where they live
is almost surely fashioned from story.
Everything is a journey away, that is

how story begins. As a child I knew
these things. Even now, aunts and cousins
step forward out of time to take us

on a picnic. In a park, by a river,
there are swings to swing on, strawberry-
rhubarb pies to eat and a white dog named Prince,

who bounds into the rowboat ahead
of everyone to claim the prow.
The river, too, has a name, "Sinissippi,"

but all else seems lost or legend. Around
the little square on 17th Street, brick houses
slowly fade. Further out, ripening fields of corn

bend before the wind, succumb to sleep.
Even tall oak trees disappear in mist.
Years later, in what is deemed the present,

one thing is left to give credence
to the town: a silver teaspoon
engraved, "Sterling, Ill. 1906."

It is her birthday. She must be nine.
That is how story begins.
Everything – a journey away.

AN OLD MAN WAITS

Pond of blue iris, sing for him.
Hill of wild lupine, waltz for him.

This is the house where he was born.
This is the house where he yearns to die.

He is old, no speech left. This
is the house, lilacs lean by the door.

Pond of wild iris, speak to him.
Hill of blue lupine, comfort him.

Tell him we weep.

ABSENCE

How swiftly
we go down to death,
meet death in the dew of the morning.

There on the table,
a glass of water,
a ripe peach, a china plate.

Were the pink roses
in bud
or unfolding?

Was there
the distant sound of a bee
drowsy in honey?

And the white phlox, did they
bend with the wind? Tell me,
when did this absence begin?

THE ANCHORED BOAT

The mast bare, sails furled
and covered, a sailboat lies
at anchor, empty. The boat
tugs at its line, prow

to the wind, the gentle
slip-slap of waves.
The white hull shines
in the sun, signally

alert. Ready.
The owners, absent,
are missing this last
good day of August,

missing the seamless match
of summer and desire,
the blue shimmer of a lake,
the mountains conjured in green

and this steady and fair wind.
Now, the crowd gone, there is only
a toddler wading, his father,
and an old man toweling off.

THE LOON ON FRENCHMAN'S BAY

Offshore, in pond-like calm,
a loon preens himself, black feathers
glistening in the morning sun,
his white breast meticulous.

Riding easily, secure
in his talents, confident of the fish,
he is content to wait.

His cry, when it comes,
is not the dailiness of crows
or the gulls' restless mewing.

The tremolo rises
from some myth-bound world,
crepuscular, a cry
that circles back
through time.

Suddenly he dives, makes
a catch, surfaces, gulps,
consumes.

Then I, the other solitary,
turn and go, replete,
one fish, sieved
from the net of day,
a feast for two.

JONATHAN APPLES,
MACOUNS AND MORE

The valor of red barns
cannot hold, nor that of
covered bridges, nor the flame
of sugar maples, nor
warmth of the October sun.

To see these last things
and to see ourselves seeing them,
we drive into the country
when the foliage in Lincoln Gap
says, "Come."

For a short afternoon,
we equate the sum of the world
with pumpkins, purple asters,
baskets of apples, honey,
sumac and scarlet, but can we

be forgiven for this false equation
because, on rare days in October,
the world, viewed from Vermont,
really is round
with pumpkins, worthy of bees,

their honeycomb, and sweet
with the fragrance of wood-smoke,
a world acquainted with cider,
blessed with the willingness of apples,
wise with the inerrancy of mountains.

POSSIBLY A CROW

Something about the slow
wingbeat, the size, the print
of black upon the low gray sky;

the bird's entering, but
even more, his leaving,
an absence marked by

the sudden widening out
of space, the sky still receptive
to brush strokes of black

long after they have ended. Then,
peace, soft, akin
to a mist-like rain

and in the quiet,
the deepened need
to go on.

ALMOST NIGHT

Quick flight of a bird
across the field that lies
outstretched before the night.
Only silence in the going.

Late, late. And a cool mist rising.

Unknown the name,
unknown the color,
the only certitude,
the dark trajectory of flight.

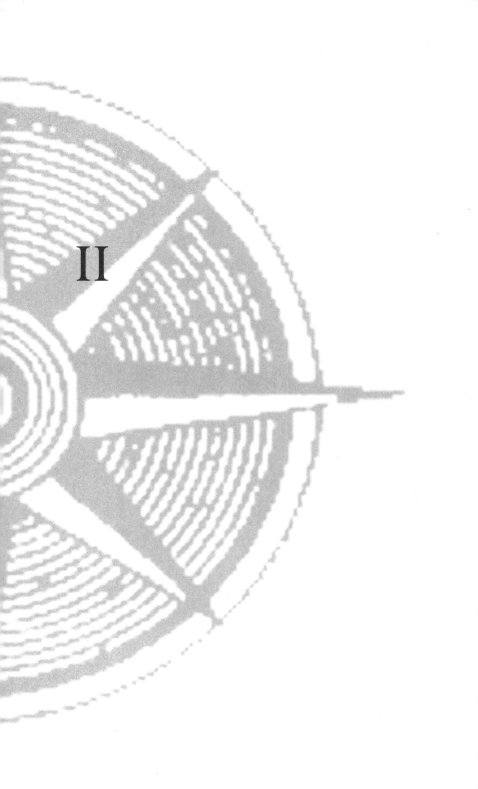

II

ONLY ONE BLOCK LONG

Everything on Center St.
is either real or imaginary
or precariously both.

Red dahlias bloom
beside imaginary stone lions.
But is mist real or

must it be rain?
And the robin who promised
the rain? The worm he listens for?

The turning? The tugging?
The swagger and swallowing?
Sometimes I grow uneasy

that I, at eighty, am imaginary
or live immersed in an equivocal
broth without even the certitude

of a bent nail. But today,
I am steadied by the raspy sound
of a lawn mower, real of course.

So I am convinced that I
am me, the octogenarian who has
lived so long on Center St., in

the shingled house without a number,
next to the house with the dog, who
fancies himself to be a wolf, diligently so.

NOW, IN MARCH

Outside, drifts of brazen snow
and the bitter hour glass of cold.

Inside, pressed against the pane,
pots of green and the first white
geranium, tenuous, unfolding.

And hidden deep within, the stubborn
candle of my will, ablaze,
steady, before that duality,
death, a February thing, and life,
which reaches out to April
and on occasion sings.

DESPITE WIND AND STRONG RAIN

I took hold of the darkness and shook it,
filling the emptiness with names:
daffodils, narcissus, jonquils,
trumpet, bi-color, cluster-flowered,
Thalia, sweet-scented, pendant,
King Alfred, Sentinel and Pinza.

Rooted in the darkness,
pushing up in search of light,
the names turned what they
looked on to yellow, apricot or white.

I remember the bright waltzes,
the fragrance, the feather-weight
of day. And we, we bore the sheen
once more. How luminous is joy.

LOOKING FOR SPRING

At the foot of Old Harbor Road,
snow banks, spattered, spoiled,
mark the place where the plows stopped.

If the snow has begun to melt,
I cannot see it, the mounds,
stolid, coarse. No red-wings yet,

only a desultory crow and the voice
of mourning doves complaining.
The maple trees have not divulged

their sweet. So how does the dialogue
of green begin? Is affirmation found
without or must it rise within?

How shall our unbinding begin?
Even now, shrouded in this
chrysalis, are we urged to sing?

RETURNING

Old farms, old barns, old weathered sheds
repeat themselves across fields
bright with dandelions. I savor

a kind of homecoming. Even a single
apple tree in May incites remembrance.
Such fragrance. No need to leave.

A company of swallows circle overhead,
possessive of sky, field, barn and me.
I tell the watchful cat, "I'm staying,"
but can I trust my heart?

OVERCAST

The day, of no great merit,
ended – a dandelion gone to seed,
minutes squandered, hours spent,
no bright gold. Yet in the ledgered

plainness of the day, overcast, common,
some subtle brush of meaning
held me. Was it those unexpected
words of thanks, or the single lilac

plunged in a paper cup,
there on a stranger's desk?
Something, a fragrance,
lingered well past dusk.

ON THEIR OWN

An old garden knows mostly
what to do. Daffodils first,
pushing their way through
wet oak leaves, faultless.

No one gives orders to forget-me-nots.
They go where they please, hugging
the edges, bordering every path
and stream. The iris, a purple

royalty, in lineage secure,
preside knowledgeably, with scarcely
a nod at old acquaintances.
And the white peonies, the Duchess

and her court? They hold forth in
June, the pages crying, "Give room.
Give room." Sometimes the roses
need urging, a shyness, a hunger,

perhaps a want of praise ...
the scholars among them
quite literary in their definition
of beauty and truth. Now,

as the clematis climbs skyward,
hand over hand, profligate in blue,
I sit by in a wicker rocker,
wildly admiring.

ALLEGRO: A MAY SONG FOR NESTING SWALLOWS AND FLUTE

Lay claim my love. This flowering
tree is ours, this sweet aperture
our home. Now the high notes,

reedy, clear. Listen. Music, dipped
in azure, ripples towards the sun.
Ascend. Ascend. Join forces

with the flute. Come breast the sky,
the gentian sky. Turn. Turn.
Scissor the fabric, release the tethered world.

SUMMER

Every solstice
should be as this one, suspended
between evening
and the slow coming on of stars,

the great bear first, then the jeweled
crown. Let every solstice pause,
linger in a meadow, imagined
or real, blue with lupine,

the fields wide, the self small,
a place afloat between this
fixed earth and the transparencies
of clouds. Give silence room,

there anger seeps away. Out of the hidden,
fireflies may come to semaphore
a blessing. Beneath the deepening sky,
bright wands and an old cartography of peace.

RECEIVE THEM

To see a single iris unfold
its purple fall or to see
a line of iris spread itself
along an old stone wall,

having its own way, while this
June day fills with the bubbly
song of wrens, I count
as no small thing. Even one

block of quarry stone, warmed
in the sun, could be enough
for a June afternoon. Simplify.
One iris, one stone, one bird.

NO RAIN
lines from a letter written in late July

The roses have gone silent, unwilling.
Phlox persist beyond all reason,
risky shades of salmon-red.
One day like another,

the heat, the fissured earth.
No one can say how long.
Yesterday I saw a small green toad,
there where the hose drips,

at the back of the garden. We held
such disparate views. He put
his hope in lassitude,
compressed himself, became a stone,

a pebble, nothing more. Then sat there,
that charlatan, in the noon
of encounter, a master of diminishment.

THIS VASE OF FLOWERS

Daisies, larkspur, lilies,
a single Peace rose, grasses,
never together before, together now.

It happens. Strangers meet
on a street corner, in a café,
at an office, around a table.

Uncertainties exist, a questionable
shade of coral, a stiffness of stalk or
leaf, the need for green, but they

find a way. They lean into
one another, out to the world.
They want you to hear what they say.

THE BEES

How desultory the bees
randomly working the garden
in warm September sun,

choosing cleome, the tip-end blossom,
then flying on to scrabble
the white-throated morning-glory

ruffed in blue. Assiduous
before the coming frost, they
fumble my purple monkshood,

crowd the crimson flower-heads
of sedum, Meteor
and Autumn Joy. Today

I tried to pick a cosmos
and was startled by a bee
wading in the golden center.

I drew back. The bee deferred
to me and I to him — etiquette,
a profitable nicety.

EVENING

Down in the woods,
a thrush repeats
the measured triads
of his flute-like song,
recounts the old rhapsodic tales
of lost serenities and peace.

As darkness deepens,
his voice grows still
and I am left
holding silence
in a thin white cup,
gold-banded,
rare.

THE SEARCHERS

A slow moon, a wide night.
Stillness like cheese, tempting.
Too quiet for dogs to
bark. Only frogs dissent.

Down in the field, a small
round house where a light flicks on.
Evening's spill of freedom
runs clear, fresh. Time to read

something old, deeper than
August. At the still point,
suddenly a noise. A raccoon
peers in.

Two searchers gaze
at one another, worlds
yet unjoined.
The raccoon turns, lowers

himself into the vat
of night. The reader takes
up his book again. And then?
Silence, stars and the cream-fed moon.

KEEPING THE SILENCE

If you listen,
you hear apples fall
and the low nasal complaint
of a nuthatch.

In the distance,
a man hammers, a dog barks,
the church bell
mingles with the cry of asters.

In the wind-dipped silence,
I hold a space apart:
the call of jays
cannot reach me.

I have become amenable
to purple, the savor of grapes,
the waning of crimson,
the fall of leaves.

Now in October,
I sing a slow song,
praising the gold
of diminishment.

A POEM OF DECEMBER

When it snowed, snowed enough
to snow me in, I slept till ten.
I ate chocolate. I wrote a poem
and wrote that poem again.

When it snowed, time,
like a flowing peasant's blouse,
was ample, easy. I stared at
Russian icons in a wondrous book,

looked straight through
to the ring of fire, the throne,
the gathered ones, the saints,
then stood on tiptoe to hear

my "yes" within. When it snowed
all was possible again.
My room was the right size.
My house was the right size

and the carols I sang were
steeped in holy knowing,
when it snowed and
snowed and snowed.

NEW YEAR'S DAY

On this, the first day of the New Year,
I'm glad to share the world
with the exuberance of geese, snow geese
flying overhead, honking as they go.

Surely a salutation is due them,
even if they are flying north,
when they should be flying south,
even if one ragged line is flying

west to no place
that makes sense,
considering the cold, the onslaught
of winter, the easy mirage of stubbled

fields of grain or green. The geese,
we assume, know what they're
doing. So we can anchor ourselves anew,
in our rightness, feet down, firmly

placed, erect, waving our caps
in the air to the geese overhead,
confident as the old year passes,
crying, "Happy New Year"

to them and to us,
not needing a straggling V formation
to teach us what matters is
"We are here! Here!"

WHEN THE SNOW CAME

it was not a matter of belief
or disbelief.

The snow fell on barns with blue
doors, roofless barns, red barns,
blind-ended barns. The snow drifted

out to stubbled fields,
then headed back again. I saw it,
I wrote it down.

The snow fell on gingerbread
porches, empty wooden swings, post-
mounted mail boxes, seed stalks, and spruces.

I know. I wrote it down. The silence
might have been a kind of singing.

The snow fell on hip roofs, flat roofs,
aerial-topped roofs, weathervanes, cupolas,
widow's walks, hay mows, and birches,
brick churches, roads that are lost,
gravestones of marble,
gravestones of granite, icefloes, and steeples.

I stood there somewhere near center:
the world and I made two. I was
writing it down –

when the snow came.

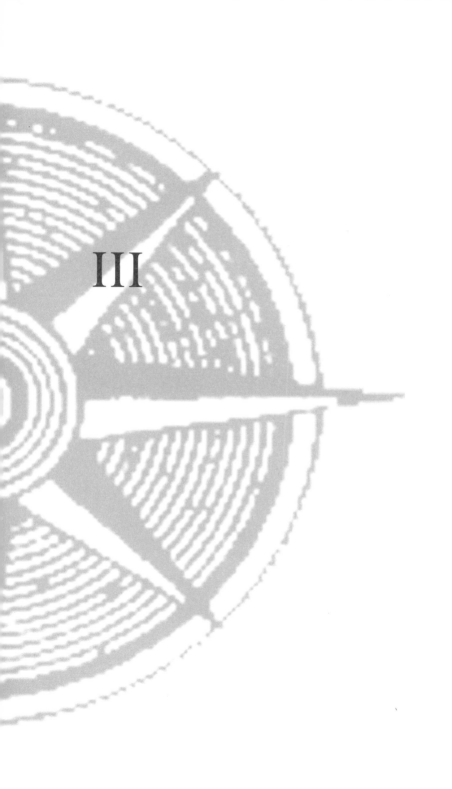

III

THE WOMEN

More women than you can imagine
eat breakfast alone
at a small table near a window
that looks out
on not much of anything.
The radio talks to them
of killings and weather.

Some of the women are smiling.
Perhaps they grow geraniums
on their windowsill, are pleased
with the color.

More women than you think
sleep in a Murphy bed. They
push the heavy frame into the wall
in the morning, lower it at night,
dress it with sheets, a blanket,
a blue-striped seersucker spread.

But this is not a lament.
They sleep well most nights.
Sometimes moonlight
falls on the rose-patterned carpet.

And there are more women than you might imagine who
take care of old men who have forgotten
the names of the women
and the names of the sons and the daughters.
These are the men who are not sure
of a spoon. Sometimes they can be told
how to hold and lift it. Other times

a spoon is a conch shell pearled
in mystery. Then the women
put bibs on the old men who cannot remember
and feed them.

Nothing here should surprise us.
More women than you imagine
teach themselves to live
in that slim space between now and tomorrow.

THERE WAS A HYPOCHONDRIAC

who saw the doctor
every day of his life.
He died at 88, but
that did not deter him.

I need a follow-up appointment,
he said, to confirm my
recent demise. The doctor's
receptionist replied, I

can give you an appointment
on Wednesday. Would morning
or afternoon be better for you?
What year, he asked, What year?

Please speak into my good
ear and tell me, what papers
must I bring and should
I notify my next of kin?

PROFILE

Describe the subject's behavior and thinking:
When alone, she would be reading, napping or eating
tangerines.

When among friends, she would be laughing,
telling a story, wondering when they would
serve dinner.

When in a strange city, she would consult
a map to locate the nearest art museum. Is it
open on Monday? Is Monday today or tomorrow?

When at a formal party, she would be looking at
her watch, wondering when she could safely
leave, if not before.

When at a wedding, she would get there early,
hoping she could remember the name of the bride.

When at a funeral, she would sit halfway down the aisle
on the left side, next to a pillar.

When in the immediate presence of death, she
would pray. Do most of the right things, as
far as she could remember them. Wonder if she
had remembered them.

When in an awkward situation, she would
talk about the excessive amount of rain in May.

When in the presence of children, she would
ask their age.

When confronted with hostility, she would
serve artichokes.

What are the subject's attitudes toward money?
Favorable. A position she has held for
some time now.

What are the subject's attitudes towards animals?
Prefers dogs without tutus, cats without
glasses. Scared of mice.

What are the subject's attitudes towards food?
Unflinching. If the menu is in French, she
lets someone else order first. Has never
been known to turn down *mousse au chocolat.*

*Describe things the subject has done that
have the most profound seriousness.*
a. Driving on the left side of the road.
b. Learning what countries require driving
   on the left side of the road.

What are the subject's attitudes towards violence?
Walks facing traffic on the opposite side of the street.
Avoids manholes. Has no reason
to believe otherwise.

What is the subject's major fear now?
That her autobiography will go on without her.

RIDING TO HOUNDS AND OTHER PAPERS

He withdrew to his family's chateau
to write essays on friendship, a subject
he had not mastered, but was certain
he could, given time and more suitable circumstances.

The peacocks, the fragrant hedge of rosemary,
the stone statue of cupid, the silent fountains,
and, of course, the hounds, these images
so surfeited his mind, that, before he knew it,

evening would come and with it, his supper,
which he always ate on the terrace ...
As the years passed, his notebooks grew fat
with discourses on friendship and similar

perils, essays which explained himself
to himself, with ample detail, lest
clarity be wanting. It was always well to
be ready, he said, and so he kept writing.

THE BAGUETTE, THE UMBRELLAS

The promised rain was mist.
Workers, half-spent, made their
way home. Nothing was clear to them
except carrying the same gray
umbrellas in the morning and bringing
them home again at night. It was tiring,

the tyranny of small things,
of indecisiveness. They
never saw Henri, we shall call
him that, who carried a freshly baked
baguette projecting from a bag,
like a long-stemmed rose to give her.

She would set a small
table, light a candelabra, and
from their window, they'd look
down on wet pavements, workers
going home, the gray umbrellas,
but not see them. Why

should they? The workers don't
look up to the lighted window
where the couple breaks the baguette,
declares the wine good. How
complex it becomes, this poetry of
umbrellas, furled and unfurled, the red

rose that was not a red rose, the
small tyrannies and endings that may
have held a beginning, everyone so
unaware. But there was one fixed
point, a fresh baguette positioned
at the center, noted in passing.

SOMEWHERE

Somewhere I mentioned
a cow, a horse and that
took care of that. So
if you ask me to name
three animals, I'll give you
an anteater snuffing along,
a giraffe and a rhino
knee deep in river water.
Nothing that's wooden.

You can, if you want, go
straight to the museum. See
The Sleeping Gypsy, his striped robe,
the silence, the lion. But I
won't be there. What did you expect?
This time, to find me?

DRIVING ROUTE 443 IN JULY

The empty road unrolls
through ribboned fields of heat.
Rounding a bend, a white farmhouse,
solitary, as if imagined,
where a woman, another woman
and a child in a wooden high chair
are seated at their evening meal
on an open porch.

What will the women remember?
the faceless sky,
the burden of heat,
some lancet of anger?

And for the meal,
for mother, for child,
or for the first star of evening,
was there thanksgiving?

WHEN HE CAME HOME

It was a long journey we had
into sorrow, if sorrow's
what you would name this life
since he returned.

Others may see it differently.
I say we had few choices,
waiting all those years,
the seasons indistinguishable

except for winter and the obliterating snow.
The city was not at fault,
nor its people, nor the sweet harbor,
nor the green reach of mountains.

All these were caught up
in their own works of loveliness
and merit, were not
called to healing.

It would be easy to lay blame,
to say the cause was without.
But was the story told
before the story began? The flaw,

in him or in me? How
secret the source of our wounding.
So when he came home, old,
half-blind, one arm maimed,

with a rage that flared out
to fist itself into his
new world of darkness,
what was I to do?

I took him in, of course:
we have what we have —
a life, part copper, part stone.

THE DUTCH LANDSCAPE IN
OUR DINING ROOM

The old mill near Wijh is circled
in silence. A ship edges into port,
soundless, while high in the old mill, a man
keeps watch. Far off, a church. No bells ring.

Three women walk towards the moorings, serene
small figures in headdress. Only the gray sea,
foam-white where it breaks on the pilings,
makes a murmuring sound. Whether lament

or song, I cannot say. The clouded sky
hoards the scarce tankards of light
to lavish upon the mill, the old bricks;
to spend on the listless sails of the ship.

Is this mean light, a light of cloud-scape
and tension, what Ruisdael willed we remember?
Monet's red poppies are not welcome here. We
sit beneath a tutelage of dark, of shadow.

A KIND OF PARCHMENT

Palimpsest, a parchment,
a tablet … also the writing
written within, in ancient
script, again and again.

Trace it with your finger,
fathom it layer by layer,
the words scraped off, then
inscribed once more, repeating

themselves. "The promise of mercy
has not been forgotten." You
hear these words…. After the
night, the long length of anger,

morning comes as a resting place,
steeped in the fragrance of phlox.
There is music, too: every
darkness requires

its own ballade. We are
led onwards by forgiveness
and the sound of Chopin's mazurkas
playing in the next room.

FROM THE OBSERVATION DECK
S.S. UNIVERSE EXPLORER
GLACIER BAY, ALASKA

The day went floating by
in urn of stone and glass.
I saw it rain upon the ice.
I heard the glaciers calve.

The parsed sky held
clouds and fog. Kittiwakes
left no mark
upon that sky,

so empty
was all space.
Once a harbor seal
asleep upon a floe ...

A humpback whale was
fluke, was plunge
and then, nothing
was at all.

We sat in upholstered
chairs, deep red,
sheltered from the winds,
the cold – our coffee

strong and black. Distanced
from the boundaries
of time, we learned
rudiments of language

for continents now gone,
islands of basaltic rock,
chronologies of loss. We
held no valid passports

for the place, can only say
the blue-white glacier milk
coursed through ice and all the world
was drift and had the list of dream.

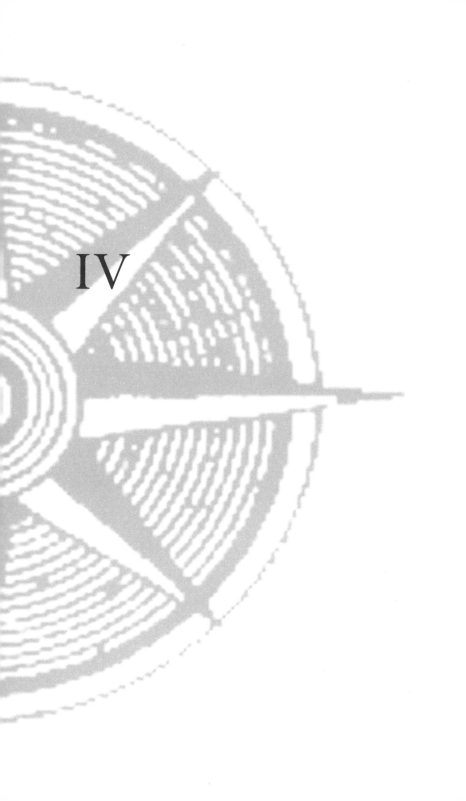

IV

NEITHER SUN NOR MOON

It must be the wind
that tears holes in the sky,
holes we can't see, hidden
behind clouds, we so unsuspecting ...

holes that eat the sweet bread
of our morning, sully the yellow
noon, soil the transparencies
of evening, then pilfer the moon,

until all that is left is the passageway
to night and our incredulity, as we
try to fathom the rent sky and a world
that has stumbled into war.

HOW THE DAY ENDED

All day, a sullen wind.
Poets culled out
metaphors, the hawk for death,
the rose for innocence, the fox

as watchfulness, while all the while
the high thin clouds
moved unnoticed towards the west.
The clouds dissembling,

one moment as flying fish,
then gliding forth as
pure white swans, returned
to some fixed point

beyond the ridge,
beyond the penciled harmony
of mountains, spruce and pine.
There at a crossing marked

by flame, they faced the real,
the fierce, the untuned
night, went down
burning.

MUTUAL

After the snow, in plunging
cold, goldfinches flock
to my feeder and I,
at the window, feed
and feast on the sight –
the world up-righted again
by so slight a thing
as thistle seed and favor.

AFTER SEPTEMBER 11TH

I wrote a poem for the world
embellished with fanfare of brass.
No one came to hear it.
Then I wrote a poem for myself,

a slender prayer of grass,
with purple clover from the fields
to mark each name in the litany
of loss. This is what we need, they

said, and so I let them take it.
Frail words, mere raft of reeds,
what are you before the rising river
of our grief and a world in need?

NEW SNOW

Always the word "after" ...
After the day, after the night,
after long hours of sifting snow,

when clearing comes and morning,
when every tree and shrub and stick
is made anew, sculpted in linen,

after the hard and angled world
loses itself in the cursive and the round,
after the transfiguring touch, we

do not want wind. In a landscape
formed of stillness, feathered in down,
we find a center, out of time.

Not even a rabbit's footfall
can be heard. Here we must risk
attentiveness to peace.

After the fresh snow, we would
stand with the trees, arms
outstretched. Please, no wind.

IN THE FIELDS

Perhaps I should mention the cows,
their black sides splotched with white,
though by now I've had enough of them,
their bellowing, their silences, their
standing in fields, facing this way and that.

As November nears, is there something here
that wills to unseat us?... the fields empty,
except for the cows, except for our questions.
Why do cows bellow? Why do they stop?
And why do we, who have choices to make,
stand in these fields, facing this way and that?

WHILE IT WAS YET DARK

   the monks arose
from their beds in the dorter,
passed through the night stair doorway,
down the night stairs to the choir
and took their appointed places.

Not one of them was ready,
the snow falling, the cold
seeping in on gray stone.
Yet, binding a holy silence
to them, shield and armor, they
thrust the darkness aside,
strong in psalms of salvation,
singing the mystery
long before the Lord
opened his hands
to show them the new day —

   so did He yearn
for them to know Him,
apart from His favors
and the seasons of His light.

MY ANSWER TO YOUR QUESTION

A snow-watcher is one
compelled to walk to the edge
of his pond to see for himself

the first flakes of the first snow
falling on water. As the snow
intensifies and the wind rakes

the pond dark, he waits
for the snow to reach his woodlot,
dress his hemlocks, bend them low.

Only then is he satisfied.
Haven't you, too, stood
on a shore and willed the squall-line

to reach you? And when it did,
were there any words you failed
to write down, words torn

from the storm and the dark,
words of feasting or sorrow?
If so, write them down now.

THINGS I SHOULD TELL YOU

The tree swallows are back.
They are nesting in the bird house,
the one near the old apple tree.

Call us the chosen ones.
Again the glint of blue-green wings,
the white breast breaching the sky,

the high circling, the swift
descent.... Today, it was strange,
I found a valentine in the garden,

blown there like an oak leaf
in November, half-wet, a drawing
made by a child, a heart

pierced by an arrow. It seemed
right, the world in such need,
that a valentine came to rest

among white hyacinths, that fragrance,
the two entwined, while overhead
swallows ribboned the morning sky.

ENCORE

What if, in some treasured
grove of trees, we built

a hall of stone and polished wood,
where Bach was played on harpsichord

and organ and all who wished
came to listen.

When it was time for encores,
Bach would follow Bach, except

for an occasional Couperin gavotte.
There might be tea and currant scones

to eat at intermission or a gallery
for strolling – old Dutch drawings,

prints. If we built this music hall
in a clearing of white birches and Bach,

all Bach, was heard on harpsichord
and organ, if no one had to say

a thing, the music resounding,
would hurting cease?

Would we accept the seeping in —
the glorias, the peace?

SEAMLESS

If I were to submit a proof of being,
I might begin with cloth,
silken, seamless, perfectly spun,
no flaws, no holes, unmarred by
moths or wanton acts of man.

I'd make a garment for you
and another one for me, embroidered,
emblazoned, the cloth dyed in
purple, as for a king. Then I'd
add a tea house, a willow,

a brook and a bird. We would
write haiku and sing of our
love. What other proof of being
would anyone need?… the twining
of morning glories, the scent of a rose?

ABOUT THE AUTHOR

Jean L. Connor has spent most of her life in New York State and Vermont. A graduate of Middlebury College and Columbia University, she worked as a librarian for over 30 years in New York State. After retiring, she began writing poetry. She attended several workshops around the country, including The Atlantic Center for the Arts where she studied with William Stafford. In 2001, she won *Passager* literary journal's poetry contest for writers over fifty. She lives and writes at Wake Robin retirement community in Shelburne, Vermont. This is her first book of poems.

IN LEGENDS, the crane stands for longevity, peace, harmony, good fortune, and fidelity. A high flyer, it is cherished for its ability to see both heaven and earth. These ancient, magnificent birds, so crucial in the wild as an "umbrella species," are now endangered and must be protected.

Passager Books is dedicated to honoring the creativity of our elders, often invisible in our society, and making public the passions of a generation vital to our survival. We invite you to help us carry out our mission.

A Cartography of Peace was designed by Dani Dennis. The text pages are set in Perpetua, designed by Eric Gill. The text paper contains 50% sugar cane and 30% post-consumer waste. Printed in an edition of 1,000 by The Stinehour Press in Lunenburg, Vermont.